Born Again & Living Up To It

Guide to Church Membership

by
Loren D.
McBain
and
L. Doward
McBain

Judson Press • Valley Forge

BORN AGAIN AND LIVING UP TO IT

Library of Congress Cataloging in Publication Data

McBain, L. Doward
  Born again and living up to it.
  1. Christian life—Baptist authors.   2. Baptists—Doctrinal and controversial works. I. McBain, Loren D., joint author. II. Title.
BV4501.2.M17   248'.48'6   75-33238
ISBN 0-8170-0657-5

Contents

A
Few Words
at the
Beginning

"Follow me!"

The words confront us and demand from us a response. And for those Christians who would dare take up their crosses to follow Jesus, new life awaits. The apostle Paul was one who experienced this new life through Christ. Years later he wrote to his friends in the church at Corinth, "If any one is in Christ, he is a new creation; the old has passed away, behold, the new has come" (2 Corinthians 5:17).

This book is written for those who aspire to become disciples of Jesus Christ. What follows is not meant to be an all-inclusive study of what Baptist Christians *believe and do,* but it is of crucial importance to you as a disciple that you understand as best you can, from whence you have come, who you are, and what by God's grace you are intended to become.

What is hoped is that as you read and study the following pages, you will come to a clearer understanding of what it means to be a true disciple—one who continually looks upon the cross to assess the cost of discipleship in daily living.

Chapter 1

On Starting Anew

If any one is in Christ, he is a new creation; the old has passed away, behold, the new has come.

—2 Corinthians 5:17

There is at least one thing you have in common with everyone everywhere. At one time in your life—at least one time—you wanted to start anew. There are many ways of saying it. It's called "beginning again," "getting a new white page," "making a New Year's resolution." Some of us would like to be born again and have a whole new life. If you are a Christian, this is exactly what happened. You have a whole new life in Christ.

The objective of this chapter is to indicate that a new life in Christ is a cooperative venture. You do your part and God does his. If you have done what you had to do to become a new person, God has done his part and you are in fact a Christian. What you did and what God did are both important. You probably will admit that, if it had been left up to you, you never would have made it. But if you had left it all up to God, you would not have been involved at all. Now we need to take a look at these different responsibilities.

Something Had to Be Done

None of us can conceive of anyone making a change for the better without feeling a deep personal need and a desire to do something about it. The Bible expresses this need in a number of different ways—we are lost; we are alone; we are helpless; we are guilty; we feel worthless; or we simply want to measure up to a standard which has been set for us by God.

The first step in your relationship with God was taken when you said: "I need the Lord." "I am not making it on my own." "I want some outside help." "My life can be better than it is."

Who Does the Converting?

One of the most misunderstood words in the Christian vernacular is the word "convert." How well I remember as a boy hearing people ask, "Have you been converted?" It wasn't until some time after I had become a Christian that I realized who really did the converting. In the New Testament, the word "convert" is always a verb meaning that one turned one's self around, the individual repented, the person outside God committed himself or herself to becoming a Christian. Conversion isn't something that God does to us, it's something that we do for ourselves. Its meaning is very close to that of the word "repent"—changing our minds, turning around, walking in the opposite direction.

In contemporary vocabulary, the idea is best covered by the word "commitment." It simply means giving ourselves wholly—mind, spirit, and body—to what we believe, to whom we believe in. If I am fully committed to Jesus as my Lord and Savior, then I am a converted person, and I did the converting. What God did in the process, he did because of my conversion and my willingness to have him control my life. It is important to sort out your responsibility from God's responsibility. He doesn't change your mind—you do. God doesn't walk into your life without an invitation, and he doesn't change your life unless you want it changed. This is the human side of salvation—conversion.

I Confess

Confessing is owning up to something you know is true. Confession can be made in several ways. First, it is a verbal thing. In your own language you openly admit to something. Confession can be a statement of faith, a belief in a body of truths, and an acknowledgment that you know someone and believe in him. The apostle Paul put it this way: "If you confess with your lips that Jesus is Lord and believe in your heart that God raised him from the dead, you will be saved" (Romans 10:9). It is a mystery that cannot be fully understood, but, biblically, confession is related to salvation. Paul says it another way: "No one can say 'Jesus is Lord' except by the Holy Spirit" (1 Corinthians 12:3).

The meaning of this seems to be that if you believe in your heart that Jesus is your Savior, if you have committed yourself to him as your Lord, you will then confess this to anyone who cares to listen.

What Did God Do?

One of the most beautiful stories ever told or written was first told by Jesus and recorded in the Gospels. We remember it as the story of the ninety and nine and the one lost sheep. On another occasion Jesus summed it up this way: "The Son of man came to seek and to save the lost" (Luke 19:10). Someone has said that if you were the only lost one in the world, Jesus would have come for you. God would have sent his Son to die for you. You see, it is one thing to say that I must choose, I must accept, I must believe, I must follow; it is quite another thing to say that Jesus came and found me. What would there be to believe if Jesus had not come into this world teaching us that God loved us, that God cared for us, and that God would forgive and help us? Another way of putting it is: God made the first move, our move was next. The important thing to note here is that if God did not come for me, I never would have been found. In fact, in a very real sense, he has been here all the time. But when Jesus came, God came in the flesh. And in looking to him, listening to him, obeying him, we realize that God cared for us enough to make the first move.

Who Saved You?

One of the marks of the inspiration of the Bible is that it is very contemporary. Concepts used two thousand years ago still have not lost their meaning. It is always important to understand them in light of today's situation and the thought forms of our own civilization. But, isn't it amazing how many words and ideas remain unchanged in our modern vernacular? For example: we still give life-saving badges to young men and women who are qualified to rescue someone from drowning. We still say, "He saved him." In the New Testament it is pointed out that sin results in death, spiritual death. One statement of this idea is, "The wages of sin is death" (Romans 6:23). If we have sinned and thus separated ourselves from fellowship with God, something has to be done about it. You and I can't do it. This is God's side of salvation. If we are genuinely sorry, who is going to take away the guilt? We can't—only God can. So we are not only saved from spiritual death, we are also saved from a kind of living death—those horrible, gnawing, destructive guilt feelings.

Lost and Found

Another word that has not changed in its meaning in all these centuries is the word "lost." Out west from time to time, some boy, girl, man, or woman is lost in the desert or up in the wilderness sections of the mountains. Unfortunately, not all of the lost people are found. The desert can be a cruel enemy in the middle of the summer. Someone wandering off in the desert can die of sunstroke or dehydration in four or five hours without water. Of course, in the forests, people can wander around and around for days without being found. Some of these stories of lost people, however, have very happy endings. If you have ever been lost anywhere, you will remember the happy ending. I was lost once as a little boy in the middle of a big city, and I can never forget my father finding me.

This experience of being lost and found is described in the story of the prodigal son. Jesus was saying that all of us, at one time or another, go into the "far country." Some folks say that this is not so much a story of a prodigal son as it is a tale of a "waiting father." According to this interpretation, the text of this story might very well be, "This my son was dead, and is alive again; he was lost, and is found" (Luke 15:24). This leads us to the next thing that God does for us in the process of salvation.

A New Life

God gives new life if we really commit ourselves. Just as you once were born as a girl child and grew to be a woman or a boy child and grew to be a man, you were, also, once born as a child of God. And if so, you should now be in the process of becoming a full-grown Christian.

Once in a while in a new members' class, especially for young people, I like to look at a young woman and ask, "Are you a girl?" and wait for the answer. Usually, it is not long. She will simply say, "I am," or "Certainly I am," or maybe, "You know I am." Then, I'll look around the room and pick out a boy and say, "Are you a boy?" and listen to him say, "Yes, I'm a boy."

You and I both know we grow to be men or women because we were born that way. This was not our doing. This all happened with the gift of life from our parents. I believe this is a solid illustration of what happens when we become Christians. We believe, we repent, we choose, we commit, and all those other things we talked about in the first part of this chapter, but the new life is a gift from God. That's why the Bible says, "By grace you have been saved through faith; and this is not your doing, it is the gift of God" (Ephesians 2:8). Anything less than a whole new life in Christ, with his Spirit coming into our lives to help and to empower, would amount to nothing more than a New Year's type resolution. Probably the greatest truth known to us under God is the truth about the Holy Spirit coming into our lives when we first believe and staying there throughout eternity. All this means the Father has put you in his family.

Some days you might break the fellowship, but the relationship remains. This doesn't mean that you are going to be sinless or never turn your back on the will of God again. It simply means that you are a child of God. You belong to the family. You will never be locked out of the house. God will always give you the key. This is something worth celebrating. We gather in our churches on Sunday morning to celebrate the presence of God in our lives all the previous week—what he helped us do and what he kept us from doing by nudging us from within.

Conclusion

Now, before moving on to the beliefs and disciplines of the Christian faith, it might be a good idea to look over this chapter as a checklist. Have any of these things or all of these things happened to you? Sort out your responsibility from God's responsibility.

Martin Luther is supposed to have said once that "a Christian should work as though everything depended on him, and pray as though everything depended on God." There is a dualism to the Christian life. As we said in the beginning, it is a cooperative venture. Since I am free to live my life as I please, I must commit myself to God before I can know what he does. Remember, God respects you. He'll not make you do any of this, nor will he do any of his work unless you will it. One concluding question: "Are you a Christian?" If you cannot answer that with conviction, you are in trouble. I would strongly suggest that you have another private interview with God and ask him what is wrong. Such interviews are best held through prayer, but reading the Bible will certainly help.

Chapter 2

I
Believe

Who Said So?

Since the Bible is our basic source book for information concerning God, the doctrine of the Word of God should be considered first. The important thing, however, is to be well aware of the place the Bible has in all of our beliefs. God spoke before anything was ever written down. The living word of God always stands behind the written word. God spoke through holy people of old and spoke in a unique way through his Son. "In many and various ways God spoke of old to our fathers by the prophets; but in these last days he has spoken to us by a Son . . ." (Hebrews 1:1-2).

Christians believe that the Bible is the Word of God but that his ultimate word was Jesus himself. Jesus' teachings were recorded by his apostles and have become a standard for faith and conduct through all the centuries since. We listen to what the church has taught us about him. We have our own experiences to inspire us, but we study the written record of his revelation in order to be sure. In the most fundamental sense, Jesus himself is our authority in everything, but the question immediately comes—how do we know his will for our lives? Of course, we pray and ask for understanding, but the Bible becomes the channel through which he speaks to us with authority.

There are many good influences upon our lives—many good teachers, many great experiences—but our theology, what we believe about God and humankind, comes from the Bible.

We Start with God

There is an old truism that goes, "I am what I believe." Offhand, I can't think of anything more pertinent to a chapter on Christian doctrine than that simple truth. Everything we are and everything we do begins with what we really believe—believe about God, about humankind, about ourselves.

Let's start with God. The opening words in the Bible are, "In the beginning God . . ." (Genesis 1:1). Everything that Christians believe is rooted in their attitude toward God. The theologians have wonderful big words for God's attributes. God is all powerful, omnipotent. God is everywhere and therefore omnipresent. God knows everything, is omniscient. Probably the best definition ever written was the one-word definition by John: "God is love" (1 John 4:8, 16). This speaks of a fundamental attribute—God is a person. God not only is the creator of the systems and the universes, but is also a person who cares, who takes a personal interest in all of creation—who loves.

It might be said that all people everywhere have some kind of a God, just as all ancient civilizations have indicated a faith in an afterlife. As Christians our belief in God is that God is concerned— that God not only was there in creation but is also here now in creation.

We Make Straight for Christ

Christian beliefs are not predicated only upon the existence, reality, and presence of God. We have some very strong beliefs about the One from whom we get our name. Christians hold that Jesus is "the only begotten Son of God." The Bible teaches in Matthew and Luke that Jesus was born of the virgin Mary. The name for Jesus very frequently used in the New Testament is the "Lord Jesus Christ." We share our belief in God with many religions in the world. We share, however, only with Christians the belief in the incarnation—God in the flesh. If someone asks us what God is like, the only adequate answer has to be "God is like Jesus." (See John 14:9.)

Christians historically and universally have held that Jesus was unique—not only different from us in degree but also in kind—not only the best man who ever lived, but also the only one who fully represented God in all that he was and all that he did. If someone asks you, "What do Christians believe?" you could hardly come up with a better answer than, "They believe that Jesus is 'the Christ, the Son of the living God'" (Matthew 16:16).

The Holy Spirit

Aside from the incarnation, which we mentioned above, it may be that the doctrine of the Holy Spirit is the most extraordinary and, when understood, the most exciting part of the Christian faith. Not only was Jesus once here representing God, but while he was here, he promised us that the Spirit which was in him would be in us. For many of us, God seems so far away. We sometimes even think of Jesus as having only lived in the first century of our era. The most astounding testimony that Christians offer is that Jesus is still here. Of course, the big thing about this is that, in terms of my living under the lordship of Christ, I have outside help. Through simple childlike faith, the Spirit of Christ enters my life and I have what the Bible calls "the power of the Holy Spirit" (Romans 15:13).

One Plus One Plus One Equals Three

You would not have to be a mathematician to realize that if you add God the Creator to God the Son to God the Holy Spirit you will have three manifestations of God. Many books have been written trying to explain the Trinity—how can there be one God and three persons? However, just because the Trinity defies complete explanation is no reason to say that it does not exist.

Although the word "trinity" is not used in the New Testament, the doctrine is there in the experience of the early Christians: "The grace of the Lord Jesus Christ and the love of God and the fellowship of the Holy Spirit be with you all" (2 Corinthians 13:14). Because Christians have continued to know God in these three persons, they profess belief in the Trinity.

Salvation Is a Big Word

The Bible teaches that "all have sinned and fall short of the glory of God" (Romans 3:23). It also teaches that "by grace you have been saved through faith; and this is not your own doing, it is the gift of God" (Ephesians 2:8). There are many beautiful words in theological vocabulary for the doctrine of salvation. When you come right down to it, however, salvation is what happened to you and to me when we first believed that God was in Christ, reconciling us to himself. God forgave us. God restored us and gave us something of himself—

indeed, the very presence of his Holy Spirit, the Spirit you have just been reading about. Sometimes we call this "Christ dying for our sins." It has been called atonement—redemption. And the coming of God's Spirit into our lives has been called regeneration. Big words notwithstanding, God did something for us which we could not do for ourselves. The Bible describes this as "grace"—referred to by some as "unmerited favor." Grace is the gift of God to us. Another way of saying it is: Jesus loved us, gave himself for us, and set us free. The most inclusive term for this in the Bible is salvation, which means liberation by God to live under the lordship of Christ and with all of his people forever.

Where Do We Go from Here?

Deeply imbedded in the message of the New Testament, repeated over and over again, is the truth that the future belongs to God. As individuals we look forward to the resurrection of the body and eternal life with God. As Paul says, "If for this life only we have hoped in Christ, we are of all men most to be pitied" (1 Corinthians 15:19). But we believe not only in the resurrection of Christ, but in our own as well (see Romans 6:4).

Sometimes when things seem good, especially physically and materially, Christians tend to forget or neglect their hope. But when our security and hope in the world are threatened, we are strengthened by the knowledge that we look forward "to the city which has foundations, whose builder and maker is God" (Hebrews 11:10).

Chapter 3

The Baptists

From the very beginning seven distinctive emphases have characterized the people called Baptists. While some of these emphases are shared by other Christians, this grouping sets Baptists apart. We can understand who we are today by realizing how we came into existence and appreciating our heritage.

The New Testament—Our Creed

As a people, Baptists have no creed but the Bible, and they hold that the New Testament is God's authority for all matters of faith and conduct. The great value of this emphasis is that no handful of doctrines has been elevated above the whole body of biblical truth. Ethics—the Sermon on the Mount—are taken as seriously as beliefs—John 3:16. Much that we have done as Baptists in our witness to society has been because of this overriding conviction that the Bible is the Word of God and we are to obey it. Our history is dotted with the names of great men who dared to speak out against the evils of their time.

For example, in 1886 Walter Rauschenbusch took the gospel so seriously that, as a Baptist pastor from the section of New York City known as Hell's Kitchen, he appeared before the city council of New York to plead for playground space for the children.

All of us are aware of what Martin Luther King, Jr., did as a Baptist minister to bring love and justice in society for the black people. The impetus and great social involvement on the part of the church and its leaders did not come from following creedal statements, however ancient and important, but from taking seriously the total message of the New Testament.

Regenerate Church Membership

Baptists hold that all Christians are born from above—a new birth that comes through faith in God and his work of grace in our lives. We convert—we repent—God makes all things new. This is called the new birth. "Do not marvel that I said to you, 'You must be born anew'" (John 3:7). This new birth comes some time after the age of accountability—the age when a person is old enough to say for himself or herself, "I believe in God," and by the same token old enough to say, "I am going to run my own life, without the help of God." The important part of this Baptist emphasis, however, is the requirement that someone must be old enough for this experience before becoming a member of the church and professing faith by what we have historically called "believers' baptism."

When this doctrine of regenerate church membership is taken seriously, every member of the local church should be qualified to express personally his or her faith before the church and to give evidence of a new life in Christ.

Our church rolls, therefore, traditionally include only those who have actually professed their faith and do not include members of the family too young for this experience.

Believers' Baptism

This doctrine might not be the most important for Baptists, but it certainly has given us the most publicity. We can neither trace our lineage back to John the Baptist nor mark the time when people decided they wanted to be called Baptists. Even as followers of Christ were called Christians first at Antioch (Acts 11:26), probably by non-Christians, so the name "Baptist" was probably first given to us by non-Baptists. The reason? We dared to baptize people after they had been "baptized" as infants. Consequently, we were called anabaptists, which literally means baptizing again. But the name probably stuck because it identifies us as a people who believe that one should experience personally the presence of the Lord before becoming a part of the church and certainly before being baptized. Consequently, the emphasis from the beginning of the first English-speaking Baptist church has been on "believers' baptism." It didn't take long for those early Baptists to realize that if baptism is to symbolize the beginning of the Christian life, with Paul it should speak concerning our being "buried . . . with him by baptism . . . raised from the dead by the glory of the Father, [so] we too might walk in newness of life" (Romans 6:4).

Baptism has several beautiful meanings in the New Testament. Acts speaks of baptism "for the forgiveness of your sins" (Acts 2:38). Jesus speaks of his own baptism as an example to the rest of us (Matthew 3:15). With all of the beauty in Jesus' adult example and the symbolism of his burial and resurrection, we never should lose sight of the literal meaning of the word. The New Testament always uses "baptizo" which means "plunge, dip, immerse." Strangely enough, the word was transliterated, but was never really translated by the scholars who produced the King James Version of the Bible. Would you believe that the Great Commission literally goes like this: "Go into all the world and preach the gospel to every creature. He that believes and is immersed shall be saved" (see Mark 16:15-16)?

Baptists have always been careful not to make baptism a literal part of salvation but to insist that, if it is a symbol, it must truly symbolize something—something like your own death to the world and birth to your new life in Christ.

Priesthood of All Believers

If you are a new church member, you have just joined a church full of priests. This means we all pray to God directly through Jesus Christ, our "Great High Priest." We have no mediator between God and us except Jesus. As Christians in the local church and in our denomination, we differ only in degree and not in kind. Ministers are in church-related vocations with more time to study, counsel, visit, and preach, but with the same Holy Spirit that all other members have received. All of us as Christians are witnesses for our faith. Our clergy preach sermons and have many specialized opportunities for verbalizing the faith, but every Christian is a witness. The unspoken witness of our life is important, but there are times when we need to talk about Jesus lest other people see our good works and praise us instead of God. "Let your light so shine before men, that they may see your good works and give glory to your Father who is in heaven" (Matthew 5:16).

A Spiritual Democracy

If all of us participate in the same Holy Spirit—if all of us are priests—then our form of church government must be a democracy. Therefore, the local Baptist church has usually been called a spiritual democracy. The congregation under Christ has the last word. The words "under Christ" should be emphasized. If all of us have the same Holy Spirit, then Jesus can be Lord of the local congregation as each member seeks guidance in all our churchly discussions and decisions. Boards, committees, and ministers have delegated powers, but the congregation, under Christ, is authoritative. Over the congregation there is no superintendent or bishop or ecclesiastical authority. The local Baptist church runs its own affairs—calls and dismisses its own ministers, decides on its own budget, and then works with other Baptist churches to send missionaries throughout the world. We also do many other things in concert with churches in our denomination, including publication of church school materials and books and provision of pension plans for our retired missionaries and ministers; but whatever we do, it is as autonomous, cooperating congregations.

Freedom of Conscience

We hold that each person worships God according to the dictates of his or her own conscience. In one sense we believe that everybody could be like us in our faith and church government, but we recognize that we are a minority in the Christian family. Though we are the largest non-Catholic group in the United States, we are a very small part of the church around the world. We have a long history as a persecuted minority. This was especially true in the early days of the American colonies.

Sometimes this doctrine has been misinterpreted as meaning you could be a Baptist and believe anything you please. Of course, this is patently untrue, as indicated by all of the other distinctive principles we are discussing in this chapter. Freedom of conscience means just what we have been saying—anyone is free to be an atheist, but if one chooses to be an atheist, one really does not have a right to call oneself a Baptist.

Separation of Church and State

Roger Williams may have done more for our Baptist cause on the American scene than any other person, yet he considered himself a Baptist for less than two years. In that time, however, he defied the authorities of the state of Massachusetts—refused to pay taxes to support the state church and refused to have his children taught a faith which he did not believe. The story of his escape in the middle of the winter from the Massachusetts Colony is legendary. He later received a charter from the king of England and a grant of land which became Rhode Island. Roger Williams came from that stock of English dissenters who believed that they owed their consciences only to God and rejected all state authority over their religious beliefs and practices.

Williams dramatized the role of Baptists as separatists. A better word, however, might be dissenters, since they always have reserved the right to participate in government and speak to the government when they believe the authorities to be wrong. Separation of church and state has never really meant separating all religious influence from the halls of Congress or the executive and judicial branches of government.

An interesting chapter in our history involves the framing of our Constitution. Baptists of Virginia were particularly unhappy with the First Amendment. The Reverend John Leland led the fight which included a considerable degree of politics. At one point,[1] under his leadership, Virginia Baptists put so much pressure on the Constitutional Convention that the First Amendment was revised to give complete freedom of religion through separation of church and state.

All through the years Baptists have vigorously defended the First Amendment and to this day are usually in the forefront of any movement to block the use of public funds for the support of religious enterprises.

Who Are the American Baptists?

Baptists are not the only ones to believe in one or more of the principles mentioned already. But this particular group of emphases does characterize Baptists. Through them, Baptists have made a distinctive contribution to the whole family of God and to the American church in particular.

If these emphases identify Baptists, what is it that sets apart the American Baptists as a denomination? While a number of things are involved, one of the most important is the dedication of American Baptists to becoming involved with the whole body of Christ. American Baptists feel that any Christian is welcome at the Communion service at the Lord's table. A common phrase used just

[1] O. K. Armstrong and Marjorie M. Armstrong, *The Indomitable Baptists* (New York: Doubleday & Company, Inc., 1967), pp. 10-12.

before the breaking of the bread is: "This is the Lord's table, and no one is excluded from it by reason of national background or denominational affiliation." American Baptists carry this openness to others beyond the sanctuary to worship with other churches and to work for the common good through city, state, national, and world councils of churches. There are several names for this—ecumenism, cooperative Christianity—but we are talking about a biblical concept known as "the body of Christ," meaning we are members one of another. And no denomination or church should say to another, "I have no need of you" (1 Corinthians 12:21).

Chapter 4

Where Do I Fit In?

Perhaps the best-known of Paul's descriptions of the church is found in the analogy of the body of Christ. In an effort to call the Corinthian fellowship to a deeper sense of love and unity, he points out that "as the body is [a single unit] and has many members, and all the members of the body, though many, are one body, so it is with Christ" (see 1 Corinthians 12:12-13).

In this manner, Paul is able to stress the divine origin of this unique community of believers we call the church. As a Spirit-filled family, it is enabled to overcome any human barriers to unity. In addition, emphasis is placed upon the quality of relationships between the individual members. This community is a powerful fellowship of sharing which is so personal and experiential that this apostle of Christ can maintain, "If one member suffers, all suffer together; if one member is honored, all rejoice together" (1 Corinthians 12:26).

Now just what does this mean to you and me? As members of the body of Christ, the church, we are called out of the world to gather in Jesus' name for worship, fellowship, study, and service. Because we are members of this divinely created family, our purpose is to pursue and embody the "more excellent way" of love. This can be done only by continually acknowledging Christ as the head of the body.

But, though Christ is the head of the body, we as members of that body also have our place. "For the body does not consist of one member but of many." Paul reminds us, "If all were a single organ, where would the body be? As it is, there are many parts, yet one body. The eye cannot say to the hand, 'I have no need of you,' nor again the head to the feet, 'I have no need of you'" (1 Corinthians 12:14, 19-21). When we look at our relationship to the local church, this same truth prevails. For, in like manner, the pastor cannot say to the custodian, "I have no need of you." Nor can members of the youth fellowship say to the elderly, "We have no need of you." For each of us has been given a place within God's family, in order that we might encourage one another and build one another up in love. We are part of a spiritual community of caring where every individual, employing the gifts God has entrusted to that person, proclaims and becomes the visible embodiment of God's good news in Christ.

Paul goes on to speak of "workers of miracles, then healers, helpers, administrators, speakers in various kinds of tongues" (1 Corinthians 12:28). He is not presenting an exhaustive list of gifts and tasks within the church. Among others we might add teachers, secretaries, custodians, choir members, and ushers. We all are called to use our gifts "to equip the saints for the work of the ministry, for building up the body of Christ" (Ephesians 4:12). That is, we are to use our gifts to aid all of the members of the church in carrying on the work of the ministry which is nourishing and strengthening the body of Christ.

Chapter 5

Good News: God Needs Us!

There is a purpose for which God has brought us together as a Christian family in the body of Christ. It is so that he might scatter us back into the world again to be his ambassadors of goodwill. We have been commissioned by Christ to proclaim and practice the "Good News." We are to live evangelistically so that the world might come to know, experience, and commit itself to the saving work of Jesus Christ. "Jesus said to them again, 'Peace be with you. As the Father has sent me, even so I send you'" (John 20:21).

There are moments in life when each person senses a special mission. For each one, and especially for the Christian disciple, this is the most important experience in life: something is asked of me.

Jesus understood and responded uniquely to God's call. He acknowledged that the Spirit of the Lord was upon him in order that he might ". . . preach good news to the poor . . . proclaim release to the captives and recovering of sight to the blind, to set at liberty those who are oppressed . . ." (Luke 4:18).

God needs us to work with him for the ultimate redemption of the world. Christ reconciled us to himself and ". . . gave us the ministry of reconciliation" (2 Corinthians 5:18). As Christians we are to become not only the bearers of truth in Jesus' name, but also agents of God's redeeming love in the world. Our job is to work within the very relationships, groups, systems, and institutions that make up our world. We, too, must be involved in the processes that proclaim good news to those in need.

Many Christians, at one time or another, have suffered under the illusion that if God wants to use them, they had better put their houses up for sale, pack their bags, and get ready to be sent into a far country. More often than not, God simply calls us to himself, fills us with the Spirit, and sends us right back where we came from to be Good News ambassadors. Though we need to spread God's love far and wide, for that is the task of the church, as individual disciples we also need to learn how to love as Christ would have us love, right where we are.

The man who had been freed from the power of many demons begged Jesus for the privilege of traveling with him. Rather, he was sent away with the words, "Return to your home, and declare how much God has done for you . . ." (Luke 8:39). Then the man went away, proclaiming to everyone in his own hometown what Jesus had done for him.

In Paul's way of thinking about the church, God needs all kinds of people to be in all kinds of places, for if everyone were an overseas missionary, where would the rest of the body be?

Indeed, we become the church in the world. Whether we are doctors, housewives, secretaries, lawyers, garbage collectors, students, or clerks, we will be given numerous opportunities to make God's presence known and his powers felt. The term "evangelistic life-style" has been developed to describe the kind of life that is witness to the reconciliation offered by Christ. To follow an evangelistic life-style means that we bring all of life under the lordship of Christ—our social life, economic life, political life, and every relationship in which we are involved.

Jesus used a parable to describe the last judgment. In that parable, those who were being judged asked, "But when did we see you in need?" Jesus answered: "I was hungry and you gave me no food, I was thirsty and you gave me no drink, I was a stranger and you did not welcome me, naked and you did not clothe me, sick and in prison and you did not visit me" (Matthew 25:42-43).

Another way of expressing this concern could be:

"I was the lonely man who worked beside you, and you were too busy to give me your hand in friendship.

"I was the middle-aged housewife next door who was estranged from her husband, and you refused to get involved and offer me hope in God's power to forgive and reconcile.

"I was the young boy trying to grow up in the ghetto of your town, and you turned your back on me when I cried out for justice and an opportunity to become a man.

"I was your neighbor in another land, struggling for freedom and dignity, and you isolated yourself from my plight by staying in your own secure part of the world."

By following our Lord's example, we will be encouraged to set high personal standards of ethical behavior that witness to institutions as well as to individuals. We will endeavor to become agents of reconciliation, bringing together entire nations as well as members of our own families. In fact, we will want to involve ourselves as Christ's disciples in *any* process that seeks justice, corrects oppression, and defends the right of all persons to find fulfillment in life. God continues to speak to us through Jesus, who not only lived a life of service and self-service, but also called each would-be disciple to "Follow me."

Chapter 6

Growing Up in Christ

How often have you seen in another person or experienced yourself a once vibrant and enthusiastic faith, only to see that faith soon fade into nightmarish periods of frustration, depression, and hopelessness? What has happened in most situations like these is that the Christian disciple has forgotten that real growth in the Lord requires a continuing commitment to the "disciplines" of the faith—Bible study, prayer, church fellowship, stewardship, and personal witness. When the Christian actively seeks to develop these disciplines, then and only then can he or she experience the real joy of living within God's favor and sharing the blessings of new life in Christ.

A national wire service carried this headline: "Man Sues His Church; Wants Donations Back!" The story that followed told of a Miami man who said he didn't get the blessings, benefits, and rewards he was promised and, therefore, had sued his former church for the return of eight hundred dollars in donations.

In a handwritten suit filed in the county court, the man said:

On September 7, I delivered $800.00 of my savings to the ___________ Baptist Church in response to the pastor's promise that blessings, benefits and rewards would come to a person who did tithe 10 percent of their wealth. I did not and have not received these benefits.

He declined to indicate further what blessings he had expected, saying, "That's between me and the church."

Paul reminded the disciples at Colossae that continued blessings could be experienced only by "rooting and building" their lives firmly in Christ. For just as they once trusted Christ to save them, now they must live daily in vital union with him (Colossians 2:6-7). We too must build our lives firmly in Christ, growing up in him through study, prayer, fellowship, stewardship, and witness!

Listening to God Speak

One of the habits that we as God's children should develop early in life is that of listening to God on a regular basis. Too many people have a tendency to turn to God only in moments of crisis, when other help has failed and all hope seems lost. God wants to speak freely with us and be heard each and every day. Through our continuous study of the Bible, God can share his thoughts with us, revealing new truths and giving us direction for each new day.

The psalmist expressed the value of study in God's Word when he said, "Thy word is a lamp to my feet and a light to my path" (Psalm 119:105).

When Paul was explaining the new life in Christ to the Colossian church, he expressed the hope that they would allow the word of Christ to "dwell in [them] richly," so that they might "teach and admonish one another in all wisdom" (Colossians 3:16).

Jesus assured his disciples that "if a man loves me, he will keep my word, and my Father will love him, and we will come to him and make our home with him" (John 14:23).

Each of these references underscores the value and importance of regular study in God's Word. As you and I search for greater understanding about God, his world, and our place in it, it is most important that we read and study the Bible daily, so that like the psalmist we might honestly declare: "I have laid up thy word in my heart, that I might not sin against thee" (Psalm 119:11).

Keeping the Lines Open

If two people are walking down a road together, and only one is talking, real fellowship cannot take place. True friendship cannot be created or enriched when only one is giving. So it is in our relationship with God. He communicates directly to us through his Word, and we speak directly to him through prayer. Prayer is God's way of offering a meaningful relationship that will supply all our needs. Through the power of his Spirit, God has created a situation where real dialogue takes place between Creator and creation.

Jesus continually acknowledged his dependence on God by developing his own personal prayer life. He kept the lines of communication open by spending many moments in private conversation, seeking to know the will of his Father.

We, too, need to develop this kind of relationship with God, especially because he wants us to come to him whatever our situation or need. For whoever asks shall receive, whoever seeks, finds, and whoever knocks will have it opened up unto them (see Matthew 7:7-11). We are encouraged to come to God in prayer to confess our sins, to thank him for the blessings of the day, to pray for others in need, and to seek guidance and strength for the situations that we face.

Paul says to pray constantly (1 Thessalonians 5:17). Jesus teaches us how to pray (see Matthew 6:5-13). And, if that isn't enough, if at any moment we don't know what to pray for, "the Spirit himself intercedes" on our behalf (Romans 8:26).

Getting Together

One of the greatest blessings of the new life in Christ is Christian fellowship. Yet, how few Christians take full advantage of real Christian community! When an ember becomes separated from the fire, it soon dies. So it is with individual disciples who separate themselves from the larger body of church fellowship. They soon find that maintaining a live and growing faith becomes a very difficult task.

Jesus never took for granted the aid and comfort that he received from those who traveled with him. He admitted his need for companionship and continuously gathered with those who wished to learn from him for worship, study, prayer, and fellowship.

In recognition of the value of regularly gathering together with our Christian friends, the Bible challenges us to consider how we can stir one another up to love and to do good works, ". . . not neglecting to meet together, as is the habit of some . . ." (Hebrews 10:24-25).

Every Christian church provides a number of opportunities for fellowship and growth. Perfect attendance at all the church's functions is not necessarily the goal of our discipleship. But responsible participation in our church community will expose us to opportunities for real and vital Christian growth.

Sharing the Load

One of the concrete ways we can thank God for his "inexpressible gift" of Jesus Christ (2 Corinthians 9:15) is to recognize the responsibility he has given to us.

Christian disciples will be held accountable for all that God has given to them—their life, body, time, talents, and money. Recently, we have even become aware of our need to act as stewards for the earth on which we live and for the universe which we explore.

One of the difficult areas that every Christian seems to encounter is that of determining the amount of financial support that is required by God to continue the Lord's work. The Bible teaches that the standard of giving for all of God's people is 10 percent, a tithe, of income (Malachi 3:10). A tithe is *not the goal* of Christian giving, but only *the place to start* when responding to our Lord's needs. For "every one to whom much is given, of him will much be required..." (Luke 12:48).

Looking at this truth from another perspective: where our hearts are, there will our financial support be also. If we love God and are truly thankful, we will *want* to be a part of the building of his church. We will *want* to assist in the ministry that spreads the "Good News" both near and far. We will *want* to love, because "he first loved us" (1 John 4:19).

Considering the fact that Christ gave his whole life for each of us, what he asks from us in return seems but a small amount to give. Were we even to give all that we have, our debt could not be repaid.

"Who then is the faithful and wise steward . . .?" (Luke 12:42).

Spreading the Word

It was obvious to all those around them in the first century A.D. that Christ's disciples were radically changed people. Not only did they look and act differently, but they could not keep from telling others about the love of God through Christ Jesus. As a result of their overflowing hearts, they went from town to town, door to door, telling others about their Lord. They had been filled with God's Spirit and empowered to be Christ's witnesses to the ends of the earth (Acts 1:8).

And this is our task: winning others one by one to God through Jesus Christ, making "disciples of all nations . . ." (Matthew 28:19).

As we follow an evangelistic life-style, we will be telling others what Christ has done for us, showing others the meaning of God's love through our actions, and by our own example leading others to make their own personal commitment to Jesus Christ as Lord.

In Conclusion

And there you have it! By now you must know that this book cannot include all of what it means to be a Christian. We have only scratched the surface concerning the imperatives of our faith as witnessing, working disciples.

As you have no doubt noted, this book deals with what we believe and what we do, since discipleship obviously includes both.

If this were a theological volume, we would call these divisions doctrinal and relational. Sometimes these are referred to as the vertical and horizontal dimensions of the Christian life. You cannot have one without the other. "Forgive us as we have forgiven" is a literal translation of the Lord's Prayer.

It is hoped that this book will help in strengthening your faith and your knowledge concerning God and at the same time provide some impetus for stronger relationships with other persons within the church and throughout the world. This kind of discipleship will be costly but worth the price.